SOUND INNOVATIONS

SOUND DEVELOPMENT

Warm-up Exercises for Tone and Technique

ADVANCED STRING ORCHESTRA

Bob **PHILLIPS** | Kirk **MOSS**

Sound Innovations: Sound Development continues the emphasis on playing with a characteristic beautiful sound. What goes into producing this sound is broken into four levels, consistent with the revolutionary Sound Innovations structure: **(1) Sound Tone; (2) Sound Bowings; (3) Sound Shifting; and (4) Sound Scales and Arpeggios.** The levels can be used in the order that is best for your development, whether that means as individual warm-ups or as structured units. Video demonstrations of key skills are indicated by and can be viewed at alfred.com/SoundDevelopmentVideo.

Level 1: Sound Tone
More than just scales and arpeggios, this method builds sequences upon some of the most important variables of sound: bowing lanes, bow weight, and bow speed. Detailed refinement of these concepts includes advanced exercises, excerpts, and chorales.

Level 2: Sound Bowings
A string player's right-hand technique is often called his or her voice. Refinement of martelé, collé, spiccato, hooked bowing, portato, ricochet and the col legno stroke is developed in exercises and excerpts. Double stops and chords are sequentially presented. Level 2 can be studied sequentially or as repertoire requires.

Level 3: Sound Shifting
Shifting technique is expanded using finger patterns. This level contains an extremely thorough unison presentation of 1st through 7th positions for all instruments, making it easy to teach and learn shifting in a heterogeneous class as well as a private studio. Thumb position, tenor clef, treble clef, and 8va are all introduced.

Level 4: Sound Scales and Arpeggios
Three-octave scales, arpeggios, and broken thirds are presented in all keys. The innovative format is flexible, allowing each section or player to play one, two, or three octaves while the ensemble plays the same or different octaves. Fingerings are idiomatic and carefully marked for each instrument.

Alfred

© 2013 Alfred Music Publishing Co., Inc.
Sound Innovations™ is a trademark of Alfred Music Publishing Co., Inc.
All Rights Reserved including Public Performance

ISBN-10: 0-7390-9702-4
ISBN-13: 978-0-7390-9702-1

Instrument photos courtesy of Yamaha Corporation of America Band & Orchestral Division

Level 1: Sound Tone
Bowing Lanes

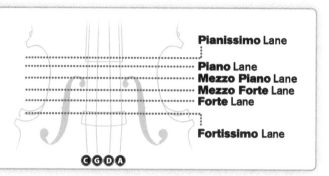

A **BOWING LANE** is the area between the fingerboard and bridge where the bow is placed:

 View video (Bowing Lanes) at alfred.com/SoundDevelopmentVideo

Pianissimo Lane
Piano Lane
Mezzo Piano Lane
Mezzo Forte Lane
Forte Lane
Fortissimo Lane

1 **CHANGING BOWING LANES**—*Move your bow to the new bowing lane during each dynamic change.*

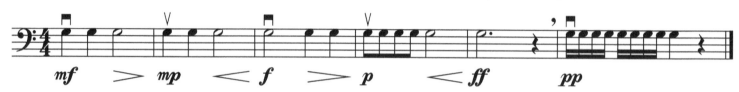

2 **CHANGING BOWING LANES IN ONE BOW**—*Move your bow through all six bowing lanes in one bow. Challenge: Go back and play this exercise starting down bow.*

3 **THE DEATH OF ÅSE**—*Practice playing in all six bowing lanes. Challenge: Have a friend watch your bow to check all of the lane changes.*

Edvard Grieg

4 **SUL TASTO: SYMPHONY NO. 8**—*Sul tasto indicates to play over the fingerboard. Place your bow over the end of the fingerboard and use a very-light bow weight with a very-fast bow speed in the upper third of the bow. Listen for an airy, flute-like, sound.*

Franz Schubert

5 **SUL PONTICELLO: SYMPHONY NO. 97**—*Sul ponticello indicates to play as close to the bridge as possible. Place your bow near the bridge and listen for a bright, metallic sound.*

Joseph Haydn

Level 1: Sound Tone
Bowing Weight
▶ View video (Bow Weight) at alfred.com/SoundDevelopmentVideo

6   **HEAVY BOW WEIGHTS**—*Practice using a medium-heavy, heavy, and very-heavy bow weight by starting in the* mezzo forte (*mf*) *lane and moving to the* fortissimo (*ff*) *lane as indicated.*

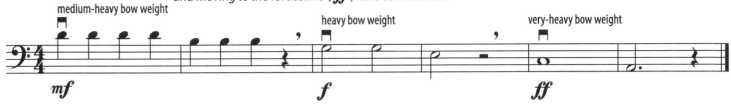

7   **LIGHT BOW WEIGHTS**—*Practice using a medium-light, light, and very-light bow weight by starting in the* mezzo piano (*mp*) *lane and moving to the* pianissimo (*pp*) *lane as indicated. Challenge: Go back and play* Heavy Bow Weights *and* Light Bow Weights *as one exercise.*

8   **WHOLE BOW EXERCISE NO. 1**—*Practice playing* forte (*f*) *at the frog and* piano (*p*) *at the tip using the whole bow. Change bow weight as needed. Challenge: Transpose this exercise by starting on a different string.*

Maia Bang

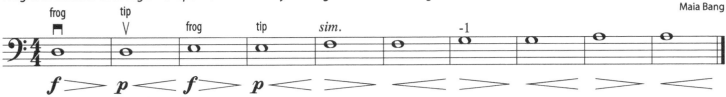

9   **WHOLE BOW EXERCISE NO. 2**—*Practice playing* piano (*p*) *at the frog and* forte (*f*) *at the tip using the whole bow. Change bow weight as needed. Challenge: Transpose this exercise by starting on a different string.*

Maia Bang

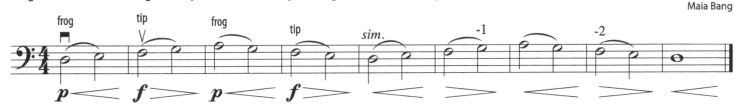

10   **WHOLE BOW EXERCISE NO. 3**—*Practice adding weight as the bow nears the tip and releasing weight as the bow nears the frog.*

Nicolas Laoureux

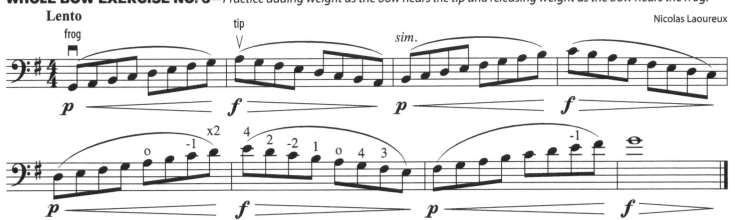

11   **WHOLE BOW EXERCISE NO. 4**—*Practice playing with an even tone. Play as many measures as possible before changing bow direction. Go back and play the exercise again starting on an up bow. Challenge: Play this exercise in one bow.*

August Casorti

Level 1: Sound Tone
Bow Speed

 View video (Bow Speed) (Bow Division) at
alfred.com/SoundDevelopmentVideo

12 FAST BOW SPEEDS—*Practice playing medium-fast, fast, and very-fast bow speeds.*

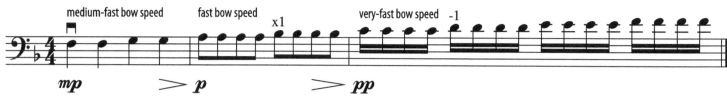

13 SLOW BOW SPEEDS—*Practice playing medium-slow, slow, and very-slow bow speeds. Challenge: Go back and play* Fast Bow Speeds *and* Slow Bow Speeds *as one exercise.*

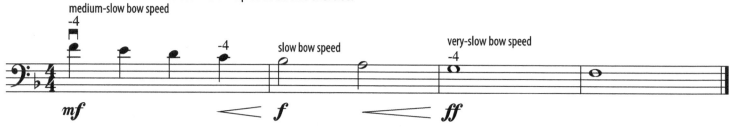

14 CRAWLING FROM FROG TO TIP ETUDE—*Practice crawling from the frog to the tip by using a faster bow speed on the down bows.*

Hans Sitt

15 CRAWLING FROM TIP TO FROG ETUDE—*Practice crawling from the tip to the frog by using a faster bow speed on the up bows. Challenge: Practice playing the third and fourth lines on this page as one exercise.*

Hans Sitt

16 INTERMEZZO—*Practice varying the bow speed as needed to create an even tone.*

Pietro Mascagni

Level 1: Sound Tone
Chorale

VIBRATO is a slight fluctuation of the pitch below and above the written note. The vibrato finger rocks back and forth rapidly around the center point of the pitch to create a beautiful sound. The forearm will look like it shakes back and forth. Vibrato will warm the sound. Review vibrato by watching (Vibrato Upper Strings) (Vibrato Lower Strings) at alfred.com/SoundDevelopmentVideo ▶

17 **CHORALE NO. 1: GOTTES SOHN IST KOMMEN**—*Listen to each voice and adjust your intonation to the other players. Use vibrato to create a beautiful tone. Violins play the* divisi *part your teacher assigns or take turns.*

Johann Sebastian Bach

18 **CHORALE NO. 2: JESU, MEINE FREUDE**—*Listen to each voice and adjust your intonation to the other players. Use vibrato to create a beautiful tone. Violins play the divisi part your teacher assigns or take turns.*

Johann Sebastian Bach

Level 2: Sound Bowings
Martelé  View video (Martelé) at
alfred.com/SoundDevelopmentVideo

19 **MARTELÉ EXERCISE**—*During each rest, pinch the bow into the string and wiggle the string back and forth ( ).* Use the martelé *stroke on each quarter note. Release the weight the instant the bow moves and listen for a "click" at the beginning.*

20 **WHOLE-BOW MARTELÉ ETUDE**—*Practice each note using a whole bow. Pinch the bow into the string to create a crisp attack. Release the sound after each* martelé *stroke. Challenge: Reverse the bowing on the repeat.*

Rodolphe Kreutzer

21 **DOTTED-EIGHTH SIXTEENTH MARTELÉ ETUDE**—*Practice each note using a whole bow. Pinch the bow into the string to create a crisp attack. Release the sound after each* martelé *stroke. Challenge: Reverse the bowing on the repeat.*

Rodolphe Kreutzer

22 **SIXTEENTH DOTTED-EIGHTH MARTELÉ ETUDE**—*Practice snapping each sixteenth note. Pinch the bow into the string to create a crisp attack. Release the sound after each* martelé *stroke. Challenge: Reverse the bowing on the repeat.*

Rodolphe Kreutzer

23 **TWO SIXTEENTHS EIGHTH MARTELÉ ETUDE**—*Practice stopping the bow before each string crossing. Pinch the bow into the string to create a crisp attack. Release the sound after each* martelé *stroke. Challenge: Reverse the bowing on the repeat.*

Rodolphe Kreutzer

24 **EIGHTH TWO SIXTEENTHS MARTELÉ ETUDE**—*Practice stopping the bow before each string crossing. Pinch the bow into the string to create a crisp attack. Release the sound after each* martelé *stroke. Challenge: Reverse the bowing on the repeat.*

Rodolphe Kreutzer

25 **TRIPLET MARTELÉ ETUDE**—*Practice stopping the bow after each three-note group. Pinch the bow into the string to create a crisp attack. Release the sound after each* martelé *stroke. Challenge: Reverse the bowing on the repeat.*

Rodolphe Kreutzer

Level 2: Sound Bowings
Double Stops

26 **PREPARING DOUBLE STOPS NO. 1**—*Practice smooth string crossings and simple double stops. Keep the bow close to the adjacent string.*

27 **PREPARING DOUBLE STOPS NO. 2**—*Practice smooth string crossings and simple double stops. Keep the bow close to the adjacent string.*

28 **PLAYING THIRDS**—*Practice playing thirds with a smooth and even tone.*

29 **PLAYING SIXTHS**—*Practice playing sixths with a smooth and even tone.*

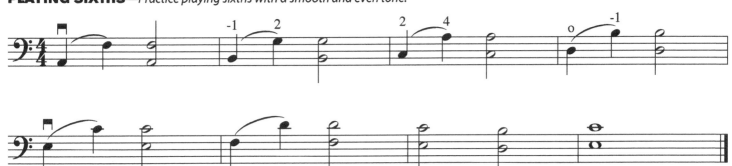

Level 2: Sound Bowings
Double Stops and Chords

30 **OCTAVES**—*Violins and violas practice octave double stops while cellos and basses practice octave leaps.*

31 **DOUBLE STOP ETUDE**—*Practice playing a melody that has a double stop accompaniment.*

Charles de Bériot

32 **CHORD EXERCISE NO. 1**—*Practice slurring double stops with two notes per bow while changing right-arm levels.*

33 **CHORD EXERCISE NO. 2**—*Practice slurring double stops while smoothly changing right-arm levels.*

34 **CHORD EXERCISE NO. 3**—*Practice slurring double stops while smoothly changing right-arm levels.*

35 **CHORD EXERCISE NO. 4**—*Practice making smooth string crossings while quickly changing right-arm levels.*

36 **CHORD EXERCISE NO. 5**—*Practice playing chords by sounding two or three lower notes simultaneously.*

Level 2: Sound Bowings

Collé

View video (Collé) at
alfred.com/SoundDevelopmentVideo

> **COLLÉ**–A sharply pinched-attack bow stroke that is lifted off the
> string in a scoop motion, sometimes called a bowed pizzicato.
> *Sound Advice:* Use finger action to lift and set the bow.

37 **COLLÉ EXERCISE**—*During the first rest, set/pinch the bow into the string in the lower third of the bow. Wiggle the string with the bow and then flick the bow off the string in a scoop-like motion.*

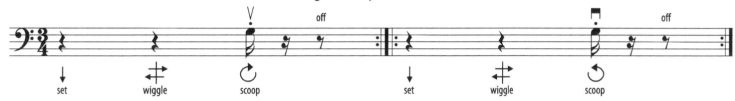

38 **COLLÉ AT THE FROG ETUDE**—*Practice* collé *at the the frog.*

Rodolphe Kreutzer

39 **COLLÉ AT THE TIP ETUDE**—*Practice* collé *at the the tip.*

Rodolphe Kreutzer

40 **COLLÉ IN THE MIDDLE ETUDE**—*Practice* collé *in the middle of the bow.*

Rodolphe Kreutzer

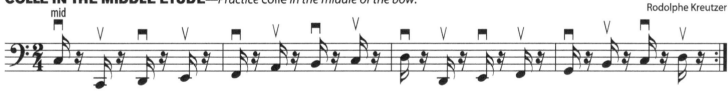

41 **COLLÉ AT THE FROG AND THE TIP ETUDE**—*Practice* collé *at the frog and tip.*

Rodolphe Kreutzer

42 **COLLÉ ALTERNATING DIRECTION ETUDE**—*Practice* collé *at the frog and tip with alternating bow direction.*

Rodolphe Kreutzer

43 **COLLÉ CHANGING ENDS OF THE BOW ETUDE**—*Practice* collé *moving between the frog and tip.*

Rodolphe Kreutzer

44 **COLLÉ CHORDS**—*Practice placing the bow on the middle string of the three-note chord at the frog (basses play double stops). Set/pinch the bow into the string until the hair catches the outer strings of the chord. Use active fingers to flick the bow off the string with a* collé *stroke. Challenge: See how long you can make the chord ring after the release.*

Level 2: Sound Bowings
Spiccato View video (Spiccato) at alfred.com/SoundDevelopmentVideo

SPICCATO–Separate bow strokes that bounce off the string, sometimes called a brush stroke. *Sound Advice:* Start on the string and gradually lift weight out of the bow allowing it to bounce in an arc-like motion (‿) over the string.

SPICCATO BOW PLACEMENTS

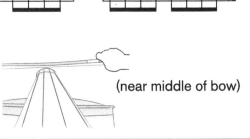

(near frog) (near balance point) (near middle of bow)

45 **COLLÉ TO SPICCATO**—*Practice each note with a collé stroke and crawl the bow from the frog to the balance point. As you near the balance point, allow the natural spring of the bow stick to take over and transition to spiccato.*

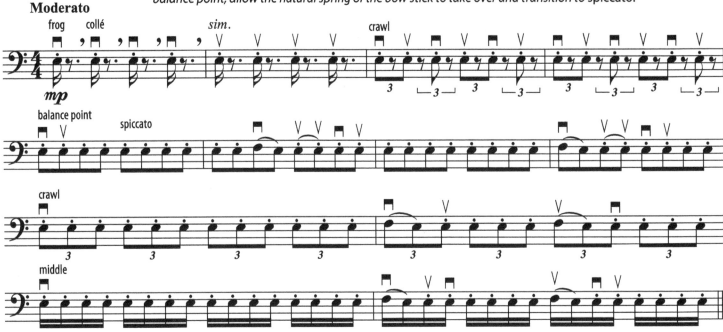

46 **PRACTICE SPICCATO NEAR THE FROG:**
LE CARNAVAL DES ANIMAUX—*Practice playing spiccato near the frog to imitate the cackling of a hen.*

Camille Saint-Saëns

47 **SPICCATO NEAR THE BALANCE POINT:**
SYMPHONY NO. 1—*Practice playing spiccato near the balance point.*

Ludwig van Beethoven

48 **SPICCATO NEAR THE MIDDLE:**
EINE KLEINE NACHTMUSIK—*Practice playing spiccato near the middle of the bow. Keep the height of the bounce close to the string.*

W. A. Mozart

Level 2: Sound Bowings
Hooked, Portato, Ricochet and Col legno Bowings

49 **HOOKED BOWING: SYMPHONY NO. 8**—*Practice stopping the bow after the dotted-eighth note to create a slight separation before the sixteenth note.*

Allegro moderato

Franz Schubert

50 **HOOKED BOWING AGAIN:**
SYMPHONY NO. 4—*Practice stopping the bow after the dotted-eighth note to create a slight separation before the sixteenth note.*

Finale: Allegro con fuoco

Piotr Ilyich Tchaikovsky

51 **PORTATO: SYMPHONY NO. 2**—*Practice the portato stroke by connecting a series of down or up bows in a singing or cantabile style. Slightly release bow weight after each note. Violins play the divisi part your teacher assigns or take turns.*

Allegretto

Jean Sibelius

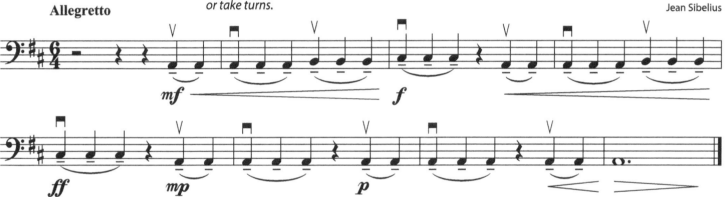

52 **RICOCHET EXERCISE**—*Practice ricochet above the middle of the bow by dropping/throwing the bow on the string until the consecutive down bows bounce in a spiccato-like manner. As the notes get faster move slightly closer to the tip.*

Moderato

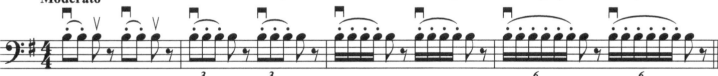

53 **RICOCHET: ESPAÑA CAÑÍ**—*Practice ricochet bowing by dropping/throwing the bow on the string. Start above the middle of the bow. Use a collé stroke for the up bows.*

Allegro moderato

Pascual Marquina Narro

54 **COL LEGNO: MARS**—*Practice col legno by turning the hair of the bow away from you and dropping the stick to create a percussive sound when the wood hits the string. Play the triplets with a ricochet stroke.*

Allegro

Gustav Holst

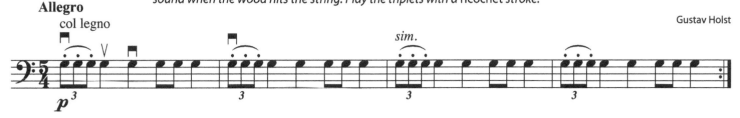

Cello Fingering Chart

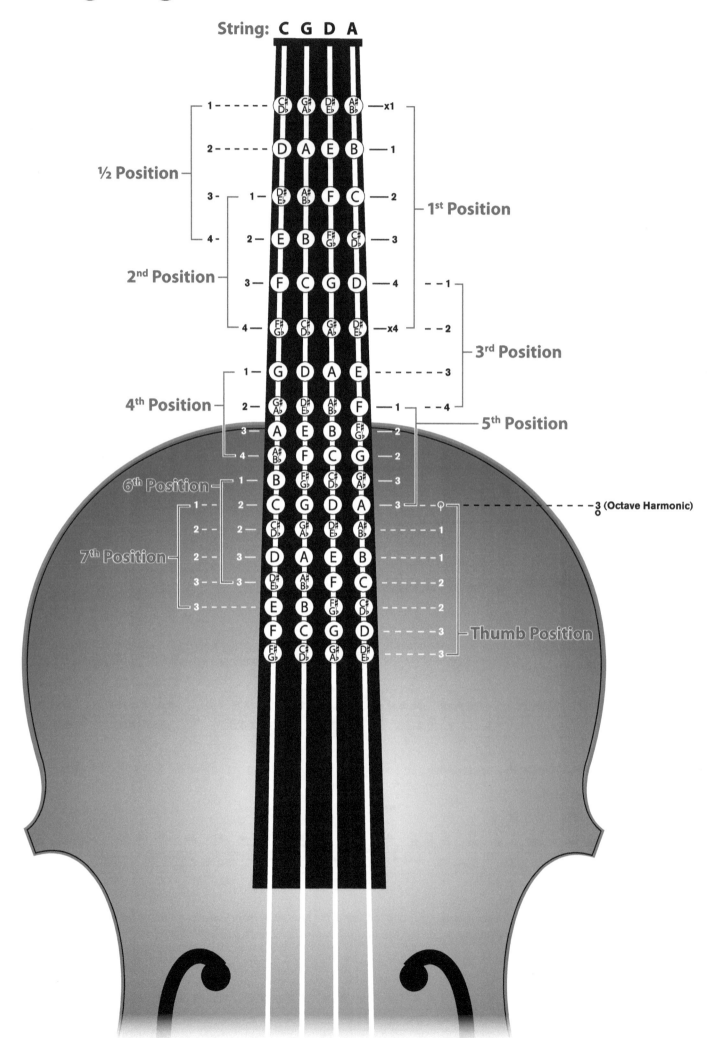

Level 3: Sound Shifting
Tenor Clef, Treble Clef, 8va and Thumb Position
Check your fingering chart for the new finger placements.

TENOR and **TREBLE** clefs are often used as pitches get higher to reduce the number of ledger lines needed. **TENOR CLEF** is used for intermediate pitches while **TREBLE CLEF** is used for higher pitches. The same F Major scale is notated in each clef.

F G A Bb C D E F   F G A Bb C D E F   F G A Bb C D E F

THUMB POSITION (♀) indicates to place the side of the left-hand thumb on the string. The left-hand thumb is released and moves from behind the neck to the fingerboard as the left elbow is raised. The string should contact the thumb between the base of the left-hand thumbnail and the joint. The left-hand first, second, and third fingertips are used to push down the string.

Cello Left-Hand Patterns

Thumb Position (Side View)   **Exercise No. 1**   **Exercise No. 2**   **Exercise No. 3**   **Exercise No. 4**

55 **THUMB POSITION**—*Cellos and basses practice placing the thumb to play in thumb position. Violins practice playing 8va while violas practice playing in treble clef.*

56 **THUMB POSITION EXERCISE NO. 1**—*Cellos and basses play in thumb position. Violins practice playing 8va while violas practice playing in treble clef.*

57 **THUMB POSITION EXERCISE NO. 2**—*Cellos and basses play in thumb position. Violins practice playing 8va while violas practice playing in treble clef.*

58 **THUMB POSITION EXERCISE NO. 3**—*Cellos and basses play in thumb position. Violins practice playing 8va while violas practice playing in treble clef.*

59 **THUMB POSITION EXERCISE NO. 4**—*Cellos and basses play in thumb position. Violins practice playing 8va while violas practice playing in treble clef.*

Level 3: Sound Shifting
Playing in 3rd Position: Using Patterns 1 and 2

View video (Shifting) at
alfred.com/SoundDevelopmentVideo

Check your fingering chart for the new finger placements.

60 **PATTERN 1 ON THE D STRING IN 3rd POSITION**—*Violins and violas play in 3rd position. Cellos play in 3rd and 4th positions. Basses play in 3rd, 4th, and 5th positions.*

61 **PATTERN 1 ON THE A STRING IN 3rd POSITION**—*Violins and violas play in 3rd position. Cellos play in 3rd and 4th positions. Basses play in 3rd, 4th, and 5th positions.*

62 **PATTERN 1 ON THE G STRING IN 3rd POSITION**—*Violins and violas play in 3rd position. Cellos play in 3rd and 4th positions. Basses play in 3rd, 4th, and 5th positions.*

63 **PATTERN 1 ON THE C AND E STRINGS IN 3rd POSITION**—*Violins and violas play in 3rd position. Cellos play in 3rd and 4th positions. Basses play in 3rd, 4th, and 5th positions.*

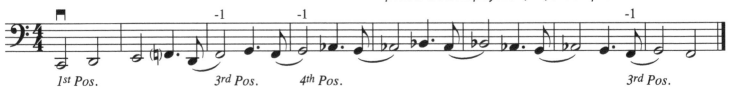

64 **PATTERN 2 ON THE D STRING IN 3rd POSITION**—*Violins and violas play in 3rd position. Cellos play in 3rd and 4th positions. Basses play in 3rd, 4th, and 5th positions.*

65 **PATTERN 2 ON THE A STRING IN 3rd POSITION**—*Violins and violas play in 3rd position. Cellos play in 3rd and 4th positions. Basses play in 3rd, 3 1/2, and 5th positions.*

66 **PATTERN 2 ON THE G STRING IN 3rd POSITION**—*Violins and violas play in 3rd position. Cellos play in 3rd and 4th positions. Basses play in 3rd, 3 1/2, and 5th positions.*

67 **PATTERN 2 ON THE C AND E STRINGS IN 3rd POSITION**—*Violins and violas play in 3rd position. Cellos play in 3rd and 4th positions. Basses play in 3rd, 3 1/2, and 5th positions.*

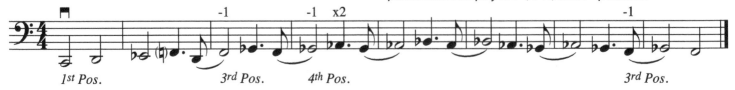

Level 3: Sound Shifting
Playing in 3ʳᵈ Position: Using Patterns 3 and 4
Check your fingering chart for the new finger placements.

68 **PATTERN 3 ON THE D STRING IN 3ʳᵈ POSITION**—*Violins and violas play in 3ʳᵈ position. Cellos play in 3ʳᵈ and 4ᵗʰ positions. Basses play in 3ʳᵈ, 4ᵗʰ, and 5ᵗʰ positions.*

69 **PATTERN 3 ON THE A STRING IN 3ʳᵈ POSITION**—*Violins and violas play in 3ʳᵈ position. Cellos play in 3ʳᵈ and 4ᵗʰ positions. Basses play in 3ʳᵈ, 4ᵗʰ, and 5ᵗʰ positions.*

70 **PATTERN 3 ON THE G STRING IN 3ʳᵈ POSITION**—*Violins and violas play in 3ʳᵈ position. Cellos play in 3ʳᵈ and 4ᵗʰ positions. Basses play in 3ʳᵈ, 4ᵗʰ, and 5ᵗʰ positions.*

71 **PATTERN 3 ON THE C AND E STRINGS IN 3ʳᵈ POSITION**—*Violins and violas play in 3ʳᵈ position. Cellos play in 3ʳᵈ and 4ᵗʰ positions. Basses play in 3ʳᵈ, 4ᵗʰ, and 5ᵗʰ positions.*

72 **PATTERN 4 ON THE D STRING IN 3ʳᵈ POSITION**—*Violins and violas play in 3ʳᵈ position. Cellos play in 3ʳᵈ, 4ᵗʰ, and 5½ positions. Basses play in 3ʳᵈ, 4ᵗʰ, and 5½ positions.*

73 **PATTERN 4 ON THE A STRING IN 3ʳᵈ POSITION**—*Violins and violas play in 3ʳᵈ position. Cellos play in 3ʳᵈ, 4ᵗʰ, and 5½ positions. Basses play in 3ʳᵈ, 4ᵗʰ, and 5½ positions.*

74 **PATTERN 4 ON THE G STRING IN 3ʳᵈ POSITION**—*Violins and violas play in 3ʳᵈ position. Cellos play in 3ʳᵈ, 4ᵗʰ, and 5½ positions. Basses play in 3ʳᵈ, 4ᵗʰ, and 5½ positions.*

75 **PATTERN 4 ON THE C AND E STRINGS IN 3ʳᵈ POSITION**—*Violins and violas play in 3ʳᵈ position. Cellos play in 3ʳᵈ, 4ᵗʰ, and 5½ positions. Basses play in 3ʳᵈ, 4ᵗʰ, and 5½ positions.*

Level 3: Sound Shifting
Playing in 4th and 5th Position: Using Pattern 3
Check your fingering chart for the new finger placements.

76 **PLAYING ON THE D STRING IN 4th POSITION**—*Violins and violas play in 3rd and 4th positions. Cellos play in 3rd, 4th, 5th and 5 1/2 positions. Basses play in 3rd, 4th, 5 1/2, and 6th positions.*

77 **PLAYING ON THE A STRING IN 4th POSITION**—*Violins and violas play in 3rd and 4th positions. Cellos play in 3rd, 4th, 5th and 5 1/2 positions. Basses play in 3rd, 4th, 5 1/2, and 6th positions.*

78 **PLAYING ON THE G STRING IN 4th POSITION**—*Violins and violas play in 3rd and 4th positions. Cellos play in 3rd, 4th, 5th, and 5 1/2 positions. Basses play in 3rd, 4th, 5 1/2, and 6th positions.*

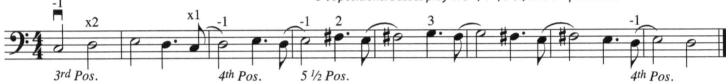

79 **PLAYING ON THE C AND E STRINGS IN 4th POSITION**—*Violins and violas play in 3rd and 4th positions. Cellos play in 3rd, 4th, 5th, and 5 1/2 positions. Basses play in 3rd, 4th, 5 1/2, and 6th positions.*

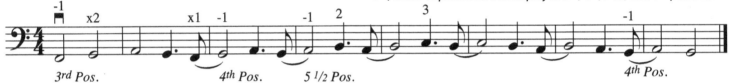

80 **PLAYING ON THE D STRING IN 5th POSITION**—*Violins and violas play in 3rd and 5th positions. Cellos play in 3rd, 5th, and 6th positions. Basses play in 3rd, 3 1/2, 5th, 6th, and 7th positions.*

81 **PLAYING ON THE A STRING IN 5th POSITION**—*Violins and violas play in 3rd and 5th positions. Cellos play in 3rd, 5th and 6th positions. Basses play in 3rd, 3 1/2, 5th, 6th, and 7th positions.*

82 **PLAYING ON THE G STRING IN 5th POSITION**—*Violins and violas play in 3rd and 5th positions. Cellos play in 3rd, 5th, and 6th positions. Basses play in 3rd, 3 1/2, 5th, 6th, and 7th positions.*

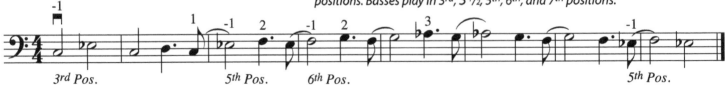

83 **PLAYING ON THE C AND E STRINGS IN 5th POSITION**—*Violins and violas play in 3rd and 5th positions. Cellos play in 3rd, 5th, and 6th positions. Basses play in 3rd, 3 1/2, 5th, 6th, and 7th positions.*

Level 3: Sound Shifting
Playing in 6th and 7th Position: Using Pattern 3
Check your fingering chart for the new finger placements.

84   **PLAYING ON THE D STRING IN 6th POSITION**—*Violins and violas play in 3rd, 5th, and 6th positions. Cellos and basses play in 3rd, 5th, 6th, and 7th positions using thumb position.*

85   **PLAYING ON THE A STRING IN 6th POSITION**—*Violins and violas play in 3rd, 5th, and 6th positions. Cellos and basses play in 3rd, 5th, 6th, and 7th positions using thumb position.*

86   **PLAYING ON THE G STRING IN 6th POSITION**—*Violins and violas play in 3rd, 5th, and 6th positions. Cellos and basses play in 3rd, 5th, 6th, and 7th positions using thumb position.*

87   **PLAYING ON THE C AND E STRINGS IN 6th POSITION**—*Violins and violas play in 3rd, 5th, and 6th positions. Cellos and basses play in 3rd, 5th, 6th, and 7th positions using thumb position.*

88   **PLAYING ON THE D STRING IN 7th POSITION**—*Violins and violas play in 3rd, 5th, and 7th positions. Cellos and basses play in 3rd, 5th, and 7th positions using thumb position.*

89   **PLAYING ON THE A STRING IN 7th POSITION**—*Violins and violas play in 3rd, 5th, and 7th positions. Cellos and basses play in 3rd, 5th, and 7th positions using thumb position.*

90   **PLAYING ON THE G STRING IN 7th POSITION**—*Violins and violas play in 3rd, 5th, and 7th positions. Cellos and basses play in 3rd, 5th, and 7th positions using thumb position.*

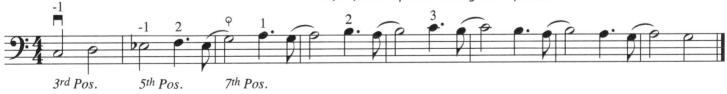

91   **PLAYING ON THE C AND E STRINGS IN 7th POSITION**—*Violins and violas play in 3rd, 5th, and 7th positions. Cellos and basses play in 3rd, 5th, and 7th positions using thumb position.*

Level 3: Sound Shifting
Playing in ½ and 2ⁿᵈ Position: Using Pattern 3
Check your fingering chart for the new finger placements.

92   **PLAYING ON THE D STRING IN ½ POSITION**—*Violins and violas play in ½ position. Cellos play in ½ and 2ⁿᵈ positions. Basses play in ½, 2ⁿᵈ, and 2 ½ positions. The lowest position is half-position, where the first finger is one half-step away from the nut.*

93   **PLAYING ON THE A STRING IN ½ POSITION**—*Violins and violas play in ½ position. Cellos play in ½ and 2ⁿᵈ positions. Basses play in ½, 2ⁿᵈ, and 2 ½ positions.*

94   **PLAYING ON THE G STRING IN ½ POSITION**—*Violins and violas play in ½ position. Cellos play in ½ and 2ⁿᵈ positions. Basses play in ½, 2ⁿᵈ, and 2 ½ positions.*

95   **PLAYING ON THE C AND E STRINGS IN ½ POSITION**—*Violins and violas play in ½ position. Cellos play in ½ and 2ⁿᵈ positions. Basses play in ½, 2ⁿᵈ, and 2 ½ positions.*

96   **PLAYING ON THE D STRING IN 2ⁿᵈ POSITION**—*Violins and violas play in 2ⁿᵈ position. Cellos and basses play in 2ⁿᵈ, 3ʳᵈ, and 4ᵗʰ positions.*

97   **PLAYING ON THE A STRING IN 2ⁿᵈ POSITION**—*Violins and violas play in 2ⁿᵈ position. Cellos and basses play in 2ⁿᵈ, 3ʳᵈ, and 4ᵗʰ positions.*

98   **PLAYING ON THE G STRING IN 2ⁿᵈ POSITION**—*Violins and violas play in 2ⁿᵈ position. Cellos and basses play in 2ⁿᵈ, 3ʳᵈ, and 4ᵗʰ positions.*

99   **PLAYING ON THE C AND E STRINGS IN 2ⁿᵈ POSITION**—*Violins and violas play in 2ⁿᵈ position. Cellos and basses play in 2ⁿᵈ, 3ʳᵈ, and 4ᵗʰ positions.*

Level 3: Sound Shifting
Playing in 1st to 7th Position: Using Pattern 3
Check your fingering chart for the new finger placements.

100   **SHIFTING ON THE G STRING**—*Practice shifting on the G string.*

Otakar Ševčík

101   **SHIFTING ON THE D STRING**—*Practice shifting on the D string.*

Otakar Ševčík

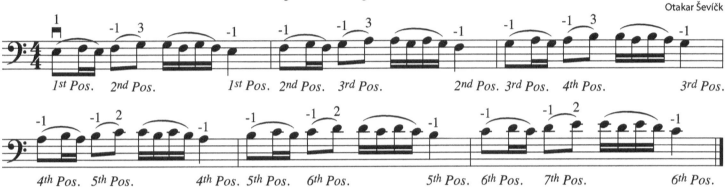

102   **SHIFTING ON THE A STRING**—*Practice shifting on the A string.*

Otakar Ševčík

103   **SHIFTING ON THE E STRING**—*Violins practice shifting on the E string. Violas and cellos play on the D and A strings. Basses play on the E and A strings. Challenge: Go back and play straight through all four exercises as one etude.*

Otakar Ševčík

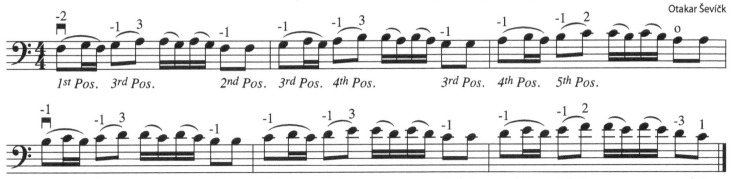

Level 4: Sound Scales and Arpeggios
C Major

(This is often required as an all-state audition scale.)

Check your fingering chart for finger placements. Mark in the half steps as directed by your teacher.

104 **C MAJOR SCALE**—*Learn the third octave of the C major scale.*

105 **C MAJOR SCALE SLURRED TWO PER BOW**—*Play the C major scale with two notes slurred per bow at ♩ = 60.*

106 **C MAJOR SCALE SLURRED FOUR PER BOW**—*Play the C major scale in a traditional pattern with four notes slurred per bow at ♩ = 60.*

107 **C MAJOR ARPEGGIO**—*Learn the third octave of the C major arpeggio.*

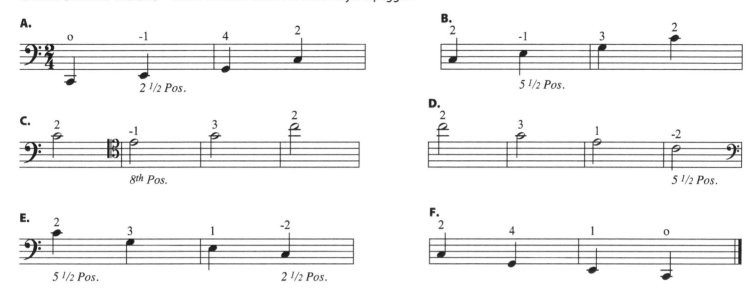

108 **C MAJOR ARPEGGIO IN QUARTER NOTES**—*Play the C major arpeggio at ♩ = 60.*

109 **C MAJOR ARPEGGIO SLURRED THREE PER BOW**—*Play the C major arpeggio with three notes slurred per bow at ♩. = 60.*

110 **C MAJOR SCALE ON ONE STRING**—*Play the C major scale on one string using one finger as indicated.*

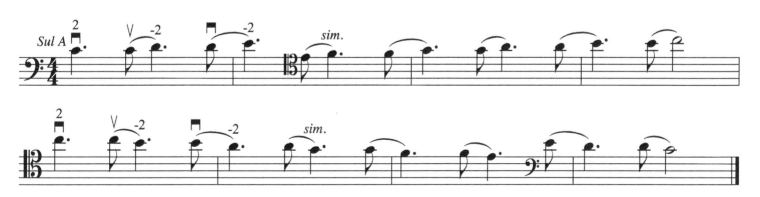

Level 4: Sound Scales and Arpeggios
C Melodic Minor

Check your fingering chart for finger placements. Mark in the half steps as directed by your teacher.

111 **C MELODIC MINOR SCALE**—*Learn the third octave of the C melodic minor scale.*

112 **C MELODIC MINOR SCALE SLURRED TWO PER BOW**—*Play the C melodic minor scale with two notes slurred per bow at ♩ = 60.*

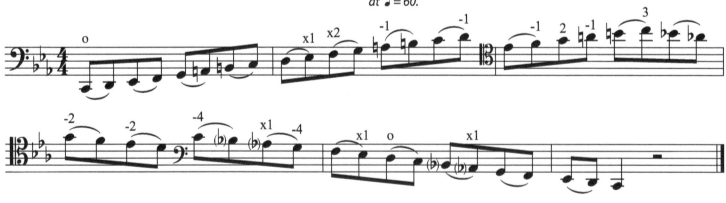

113 **C MELODIC MINOR SCALE SLURRED FOUR PER BOW**—*Play the C melodic minor scale in a traditional pattern with four notes slurred per bow at ♩ = 60.*

114 **C MINOR ARPEGGIO**—*Learn the third octave of the C minor arpeggio.*

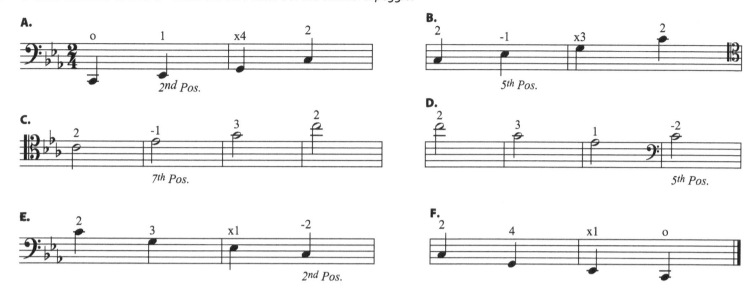

115 **C MINOR ARPEGGIO IN QUARTER NOTES**—*Play the C minor arpeggio at ♩ = 60.*

116 **C MINOR ARPEGGIO SLURRED THREE PER BOW**—*Play the C minor arpeggio with three notes slurred per bow at ♩. = 60.*

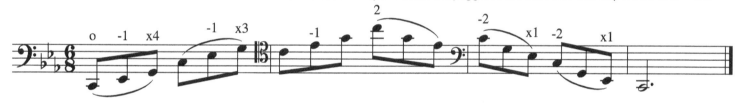

117 **C MELODIC MINOR SCALE ON ONE STRING**—*Play the C melodic minor scale on one string using one finger as indicated.*

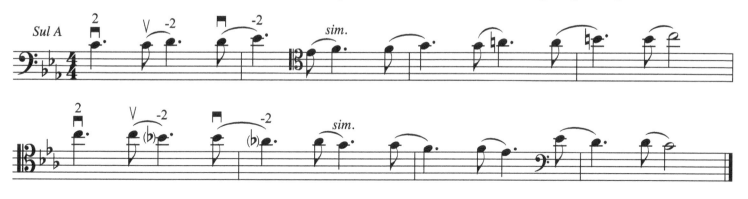

Level 4: Sound Scales and Arpeggios
D♭ Major

Check your fingering chart for finger placements. Mark in the half steps as directed by your teacher.

118 **D♭ MAJOR SCALE**—*Learn the third octave of the D♭ major scale.*

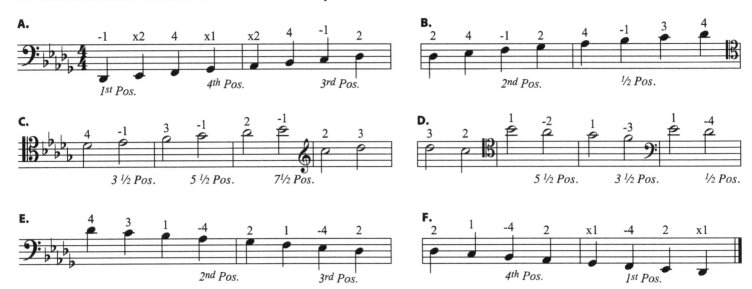

119 **D♭ MAJOR SCALE IN A TRADITIONAL PATTERN**—*Play the D♭ major scale in a traditional pattern at ♩ = 60. Add slurs as instructed by your teacher.*

120 **D♭ MAJOR ARPEGGIO**—*Play the D♭ major arpeggio at ♩ = 60.*

121 **D♭ MAJOR ARPEGGIO IN A TRADITIONAL PATTERN**—*Play the D♭ major arpeggio at ♩. = 60. Add slurs as instructed by your teacher.*

Level 4: Sound Scales and Arpeggios
C♯ Melodic Minor

Check your fingering chart for finger placements. Mark in the half steps as directed by your teacher.

122 **C♯ MELODIC MINOR SCALE**—*Learn the third octave of the C♯ melodic minor scale.*

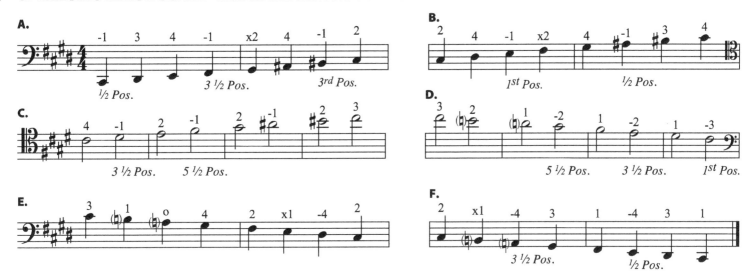

123 **C♯ MELODIC MINOR SCALE IN A TRADITIONAL PATTERN**—*Play the C♯ melodic minor scale in a traditional pattern at ♩ = 60. Add slurs as instructed by your teacher.*

124 **C♯ MINOR ARPEGGIO**—*Play the C♯ minor arpeggio at ♩ = 60.*

125 **C♯ MINOR ARPEGGIO IN A TRADITIONAL PATTERN**—*Play the C♯ minor arpeggio at ♩. = 60. Add slurs as instructed by your teacher.*

Level 4: Sound Scales and Arpeggios
D Major

Check your fingering chart for finger placements. Mark in the half steps as directed by your teacher.

126 **D MAJOR SCALE**—*Learn the third octave of the D major scale.*

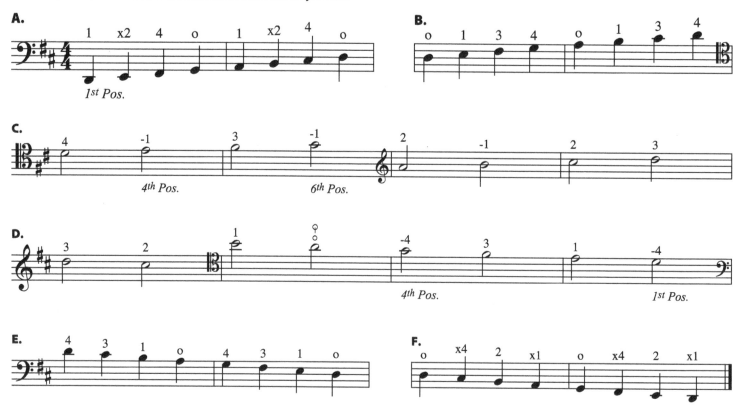

127 **D MAJOR SCALE SLURRED TWO PER BOW**—*Play the D major scale with two notes slurred per bow at ♩ = 60.*

128 **D MAJOR SCALE SLURRED FOUR PER BOW**—*Play the D major scale in a traditional pattern with four notes slurred per bow at ♩ = 60.*

129 **D MAJOR ARPEGGIO**—*Learn the third octave of the D major arpeggio.*

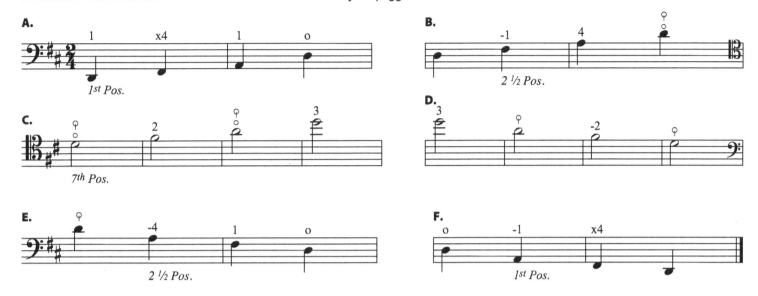

130 **D MAJOR ARPEGGIO IN QUARTER NOTES**—*Play the D major arpeggio at ♩ = 60.*

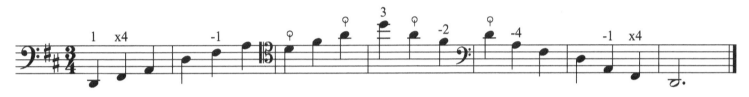

131 **D MAJOR ARPEGGIO SLURRED THREE PER BOW**—*Play the D major arpeggio with three notes slurred per bow at ♩. = 60.*

132 **D MAJOR SCALE ON ONE STRING**—*Play the D major scale on one string using one finger as indicated.*

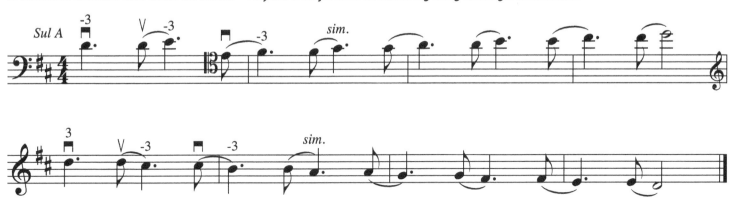

Level 4: Sound Scales and Arpeggios
D Melodic Minor

Check your fingering chart for finger placements. Mark in the half steps as directed by your teacher.

133 **D MELODIC MINOR SCALE**—*Learn the third octave of the D melodic minor scale.*

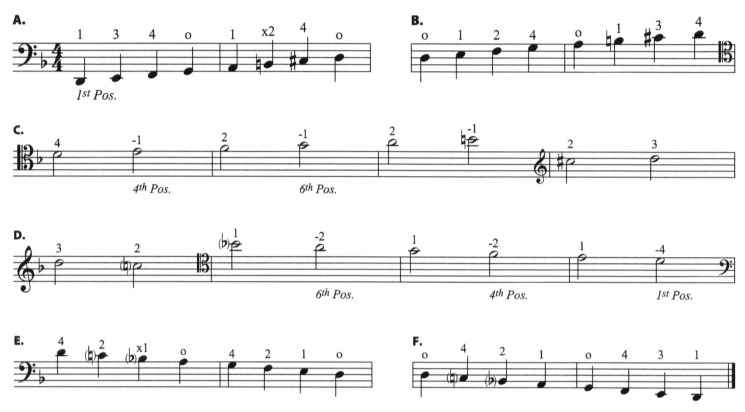

134 **D MELODIC MINOR SCALE SLURRED TWO PER BOW**—*Play the D melodic minor scale with two notes slurred per bow at ♩ = 60.*

135 **D MELODIC MINOR SCALE SLURRED FOUR PER BOW**—*Play the D melodic minor scale in a traditional pattern with four notes slurred per bow at ♩ = 60.*

136 **D MINOR ARPEGGIO**—*Learn the third octave of the D minor arpeggio.*

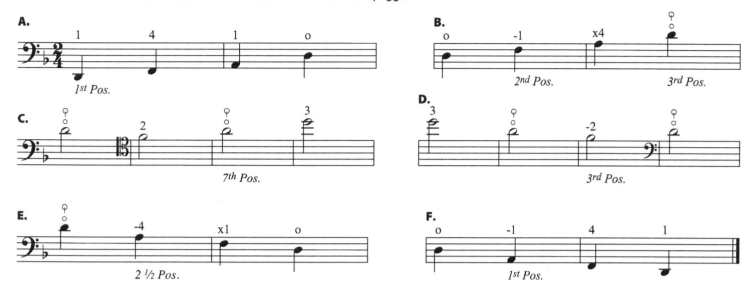

137 **D MINOR ARPEGGIO IN QUARTER NOTES**—*Play the D minor arpeggio at ♩ = 60.*

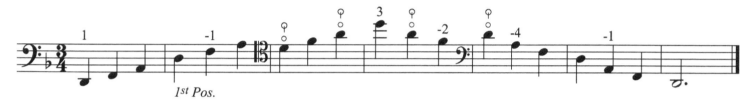

138 **D MINOR ARPEGGIO SLURRED THREE PER BOW**—*Play the D minor arpeggio with three notes slurred per bow at ♩. = 60.*

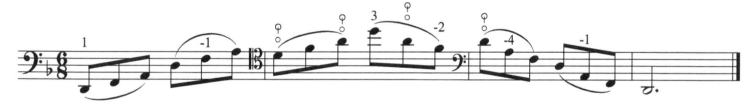

139 **D MELODIC MINOR SCALE ON ONE STRING**—*Play the D melodic minor scale on one string using one finger as indicated.*

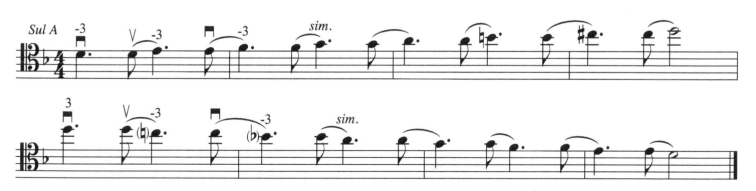

Level 4: Sound Scales and Arpeggios
E♭ Major

Check your fingering chart for finger placements. Mark in the half steps as directed by your teacher.

140 E♭ **MAJOR SCALE**—*Learn the third octave of the E♭ major scale.*

141 E♭ **MAJOR SCALE SLURRED TWO PER BOW**—*Play the E♭ major scale with two notes slurred per bow at ♩ = 60.*

142 E♭ **MAJOR SCALE SLURRED FOUR PER BOW**—*Play the E♭ major scale in a traditional pattern with four notes slurred per bow at ♩ = 60.*

143 **E♭ MAJOR ARPEGGIO**—*Learn the third octave of the E♭ major arpeggio.*

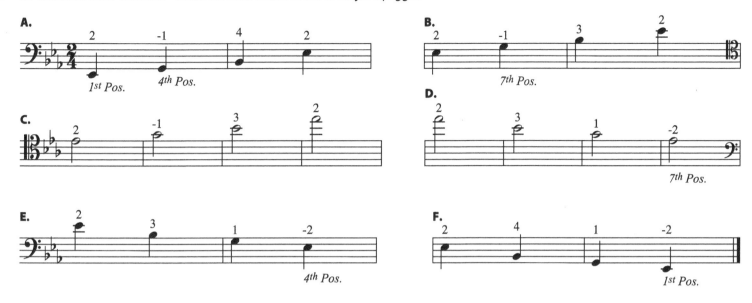

144 **E♭ MAJOR ARPEGGIO IN QUARTER NOTES**—*Play the E♭ major arpeggio at ♩ = 60.*

145 **E♭ MAJOR ARPEGGIO SLURRED THREE PER BOW**—*Play the E♭ major arpeggio with three notes slurred per bow at ♩. = 60.*

146 **E♭ MAJOR SCALE ON ONE STRING**—*Play the E♭ major scale on one string using one finger as indicated.*

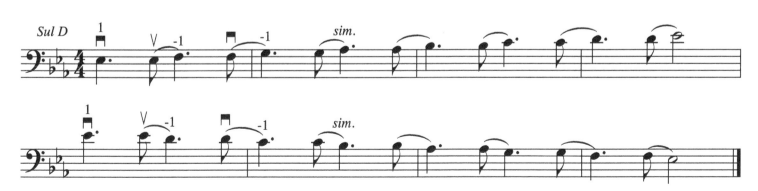

Level 4: Sound Scales and Arpeggios
E♭ Melodic Minor

Check your fingering chart for finger placements. Mark in the half steps as directed by your teacher.

147 **E♭ MELODIC MINOR SCALE**—*Learn the third octave of the E♭ melodic minor scale.*

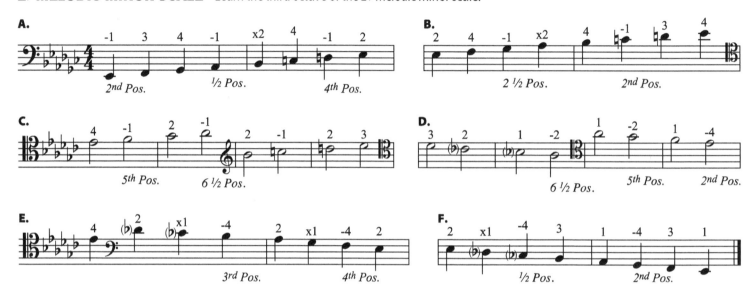

148 **E♭ MELODIC MINOR SCALE IN A TRADITIONAL PATTERN**—*Play the E♭ melodic minor scale in a traditional pattern at ♩ = 60. Add slurs as instructed by your teacher.*

149 **E♭ MINOR ARPEGGIO**—*Play the E♭ minor arpeggio at ♩ = 60.*

150 **E♭ MINOR ARPEGGIO IN A TRADITIONAL PATTERN**—*Play the E♭ minor arpeggio at ♩. = 60. Add slurs as instructed by your teacher.*

Level 4: Sound Scales and Arpeggios
E Major

Check your fingering chart for finger placements. Mark in the half steps as directed by your teacher.

151 **E MAJOR SCALE**—*Learn the third octave of the E major scale.*

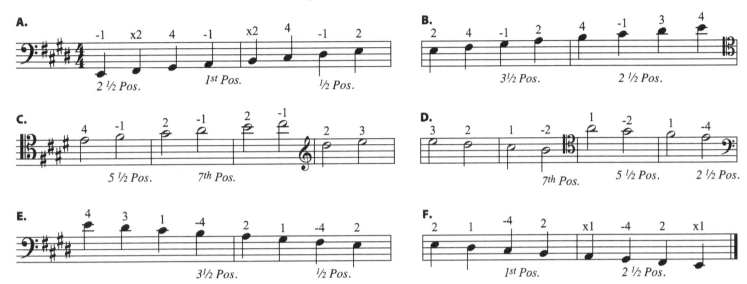

152 **E MAJOR SCALE IN A TRADITIONAL PATTERN**—*Play the E major scale in a traditional pattern at ♩ = 60. Add slurs as instructed by your teacher.*

153 **E MAJOR ARPEGGIO**—*Play the E major arpeggio at ♩ = 60.*

154 **E MAJOR ARPEGGIO SLURRED THREE PER BOW**—*Play the E major arpeggio with three notes slurred per bow at ♩. = 60.*

Level 4: Sound Scales and Arpeggios
E Melodic Minor

(This is often required as an all-state audition scale.)

Check your fingering chart for finger placements. Mark in the half steps as directed by your teacher.

155 **E MELODIC MINOR SCALE**—*Learn the third octave of the E melodic minor scale.*

156 **E MELODIC MINOR SCALE SLURRED TWO PER BOW**—*Play the E melodic minor scale with two notes slurred per bow at ♩ = 60.*

157 **E MELODIC MINOR SCALE SLURRED FOUR PER BOW**—*Play the E melodic minor scale in a traditional pattern with four notes slurred per bow at ♩ = 60.*

58 E MINOR ARPEGGIO—*Learn the third octave of the E minor arpeggio.*

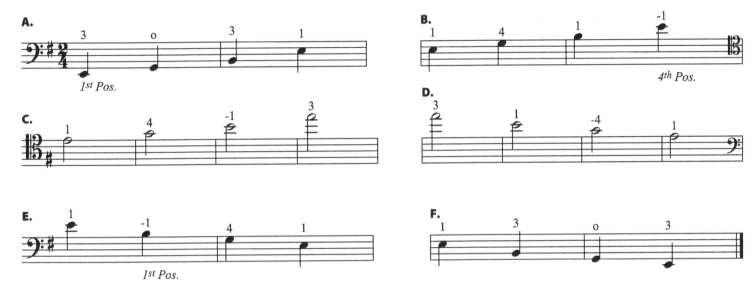

59 E MINOR ARPEGGIO IN QUARTER NOTES—*Play the E minor arpeggio at ♩ = 60.*

60 E MINOR ARPEGGIO SLURRED THREE PER BOW—*Play the E minor arpeggio with three notes slurred per bow at ♩. = 60.*

61 E MELODIC MINOR SCALE ON ONE STRING—*Play the E melodic minor scale on one string using one finger as indicated.*

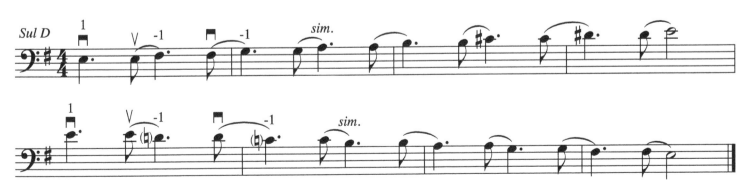

Level 4: Sound Scales and Arpeggios
F Major

(This is often required as an all-state audition scale.)

Check your fingering chart for finger placements. Mark in the half steps as directed by your teacher.

162 **F MAJOR SCALE**—*Learn the third octave of the F major scale.*

163 **F MAJOR SCALE SLURRED TWO PER BOW**—*Play the F major scale with two notes slurred per bow at* ♩ = 60.

164 **F MAJOR SCALE SLURRED FOUR PER BOW**—*Play the F major scale in a traditional pattern with four notes slurred per bow at* ♩ = 60.

165 **F MAJOR ARPEGGIO**—*Learn the third octave of the F major arpeggio.*

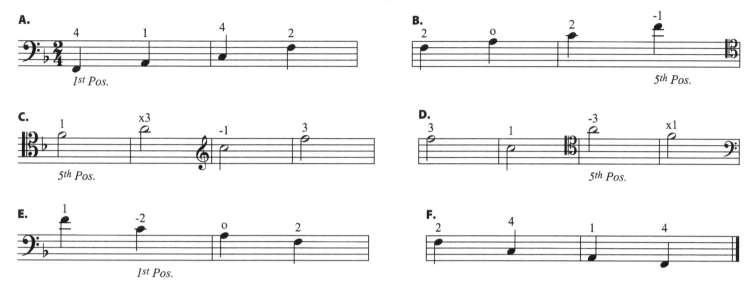

166 **F MAJOR ARPEGGIO IN QUARTER NOTES**—*Play the F major arpeggio at ♩ = 60.*

167 **F MAJOR ARPEGGIO SLURRED THREE PER BOW**—*Play the F major arpeggio with three notes slurred per bow at ♩. = 60.*

168 **F MAJOR SCALE ON ONE STRING**—*Play the F major scale on one string using one finger as indicated.*

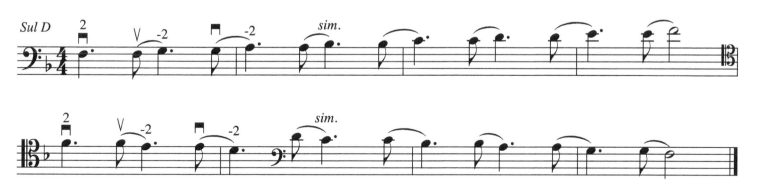

Level 4: Sound Scales and Arpeggios
F Melodic Minor

(This is often required as an all-state audition scale.)

Check your fingering chart for finger placements. Mark in the half steps as directed by your teacher.

169 **F MELODIC MINOR SCALE**—*Learn the third octave of the F melodic minor scale.*

170 **F MELODIC MINOR SCALE SLURRED TWO PER BOW**—*Play the F melodic minor scale with two notes slurred per bow at ♩ = 60.*

171 **F MELODIC MINOR SCALE SLURRED FOUR PER BOW**—*Play the F melodic minor scale in a traditional pattern with four notes slurred per bow at ♩ = 60.*

72 **F MINOR ARPEGGIO**—*Learn the third octave of the F minor arpeggio.*

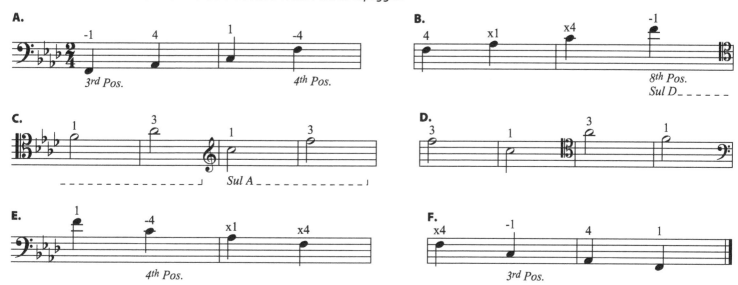

A.

3rd Pos.   4th Pos.

B.

8th Pos.
Sul D _ _ _ _ _

C.

Sul A _ _ _ _ _ _ _

D.

E.

4th Pos.

F.

3rd Pos.

73 **F MINOR ARPEGGIO IN QUARTER NOTES**—*Play the F minor arpeggio at ♩ = 60.*

Sul A _ _ _ _ _

74 **F MINOR ARPEGGIO SLURRED THREE PER BOW**—*Play the F minor arpeggio with three notes slurred per bow at ♩. = 60.*

Sul A _ _ _ _

75 **F MELODIC MINOR SCALE ON ONE STRING**—*Play the F melodic minor scale on one string using one finger as indicated.*

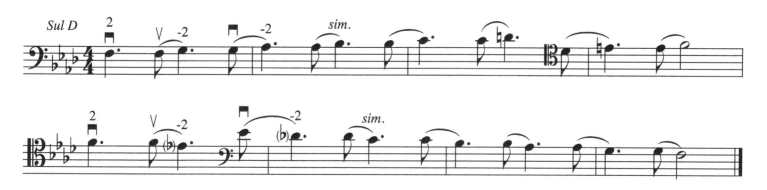

Sul D   2   V -2   sim.

Level 4: Sound Scales and Arpeggios
F♯ Major

Check your fingering chart for finger placements. Mark in the half steps as directed by your teacher.

176 F♯ MAJOR SCALE—*Learn the third octave of the F♯ major scale.*

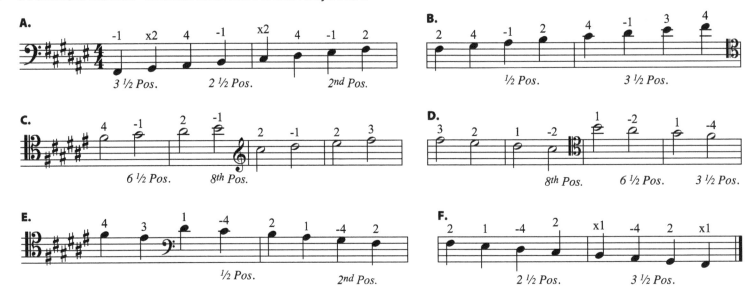

177 F♯ MAJOR SCALE IN A TRADITIONAL PATTERN—*Play the F♯ major scale in a traditional pattern at ♩ = 60. Add slurs as instructed by your teacher.*

178 F♯ MAJOR ARPEGGIO—*Play the F♯ major arpeggio at ♩ = 60.*

179 F♯ MAJOR ARPEGGIO IN A TRADITIONAL PATTERN—*Play the F♯ major arpeggio at ♩. = 60. Add slurs as instructed by your teacher.*

Level 4: Sound Scales and Arpeggios
F# Melodic Minor

Check your fingering chart for finger placements. Mark in the half steps as directed by your teacher.

180 **F# MELODIC MINOR SCALE**—*Learn the third octave of the F# melodic minor scale.*

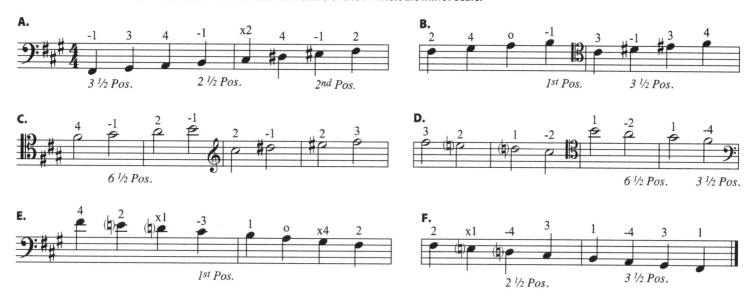

181 **F# MELODIC MINOR SCALE IN A TRADITIONAL PATTERN**—*Play the F# melodic minor scale in a traditional pattern at ♩ = 60. Add slurs as instructed by your teacher.*

182 **F# MINOR ARPEGGIO**—*Play the F# minor arpeggio at ♩ = 60.*

183 **F# MINOR ARPEGGIO IN A TRADITIONAL PATTERN**—*Play the F# minor arpeggio at ♩. = 60. Add slurs as instructed by your teacher.*

Level 4: Sound Scales and Arpeggios
G Major

(This is often required as an all-state audition scale.)

Check your fingering chart for finger placements. Mark in the half steps as directed by your teacher.

184 **G MAJOR SCALE**—*Learn the third octave of the G major scale.*

185 **G MAJOR SCALE SLURRED TWO PER BOW**—*Play the G major scale with two notes slurred per bow at ♩ = 60.*

186 **G MAJOR SCALE SLURRED FOUR PER BOW**—*Play the G major scale in a traditional pattern with four notes slurred per bow at ♩ = 60.*

87 **G MAJOR ARPEGGIO**—*Learn the third octave of the G major arpeggio.*

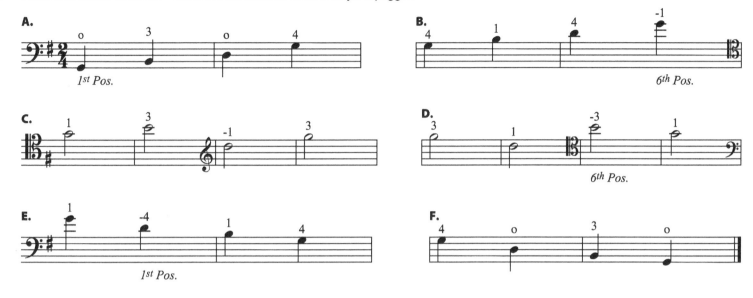

88 **G MAJOR ARPEGGIO IN QUARTER NOTES**—*Play the G major arpeggio at ♩ = 60.*

89 **G MAJOR ARPEGGIO SLURRED THREE PER BOW**—*Play the G major arpeggio with three notes slurred per bow at ♩. = 60.*

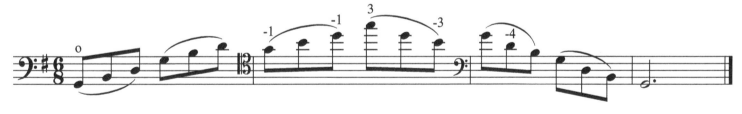

90 **G MAJOR SCALE ON ONE STRING**—*Play the G major scale on one string using one finger as indicated.*

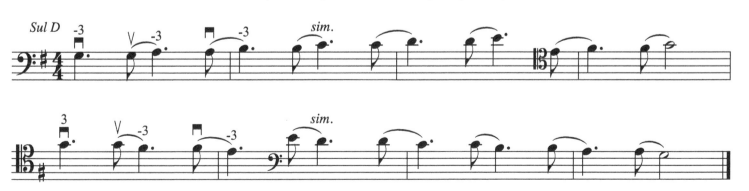

Level 4: Sound Scales and Arpeggios
G Melodic Minor

(This is often required as an all-state audition scale.)

Check your fingering chart for finger placements. Mark in the half steps as directed by your teacher.

191 **G MELODIC MINOR SCALE**—*Learn the third octave of the G melodic minor scale.*

192 **G MELODIC MINOR SCALE SLURRED TWO PER BOW**—*Play the G melodic minor scale with two notes slurred per bow at ♩ = 60.*

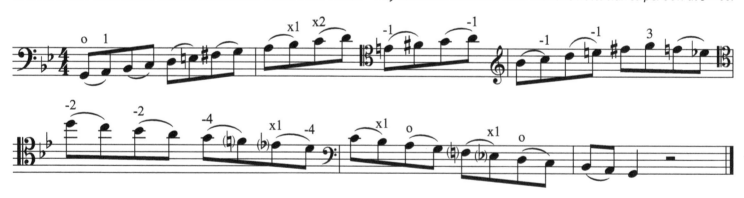

193 **G MELODIC MINOR SCALE SLURRED FOUR PER BOW**—*Play the G melodic minor scale in a traditional pattern with four notes slurred per bow at ♩ = 60.*

94 **G MINOR ARPEGGIO**—*Learn the third octave of the G minor arpeggio.*

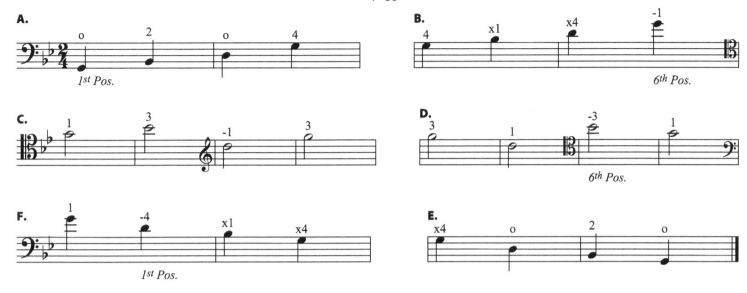

95 **G MINOR ARPEGGIO IN QUARTER NOTES**—*Play the G minor arpeggio at ♩ = 60.*

96 **G MINOR ARPEGGIO SLURRED THREE PER BOW**—*Play the G minor arpeggio with three notes slurred per bow at ♩. = 60.*

97 **G MELODIC MINOR SCALE ON ONE STRING**—*Play the G melodic minor scale on one string using one finger as indicated.*

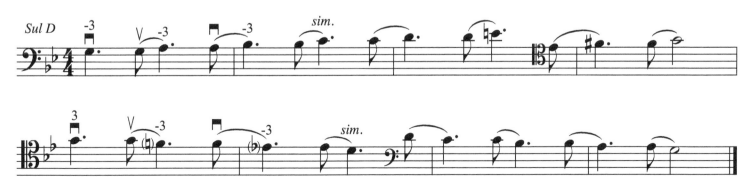

Level 4: Sound Scales and Arpeggios
A♭ Major

Check your fingering chart for finger placements. Mark in the half steps as directed by your teacher.

198 **A♭ MAJOR SCALE**—*Learn the third octave of the A♭ major scale.*

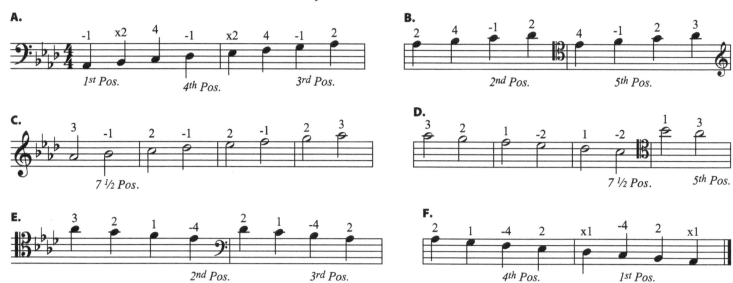

199 **A♭ MAJOR SCALE IN A TRADITIONAL PATTERN**—*Play the A♭ major scale in a traditional pattern at ♩ = 60. Add slurs as instructed by your teacher.*

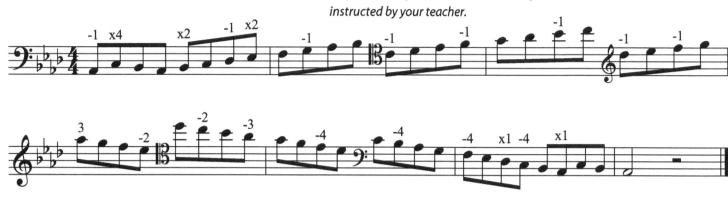

200 **A♭ MAJOR ARPEGGIO**—*Play the A♭ major arpeggio at ♩ = 60.*

201 **A♭ MAJOR ARPEGGIO IN A TRADITIONAL PATTERN**—*Play the A♭ major arpeggio at ♩. = 60. Add slurs as instructed by your teacher.*

Level 4: Sound Scales and Arpeggios
G♯ Melodic Minor

Check your fingering chart for finger placements. Mark in the half steps as directed by your teacher.

202 **G♯ MELODIC MINOR SCALE**—*Learn the third octave of the G♯ melodic minor scale.*

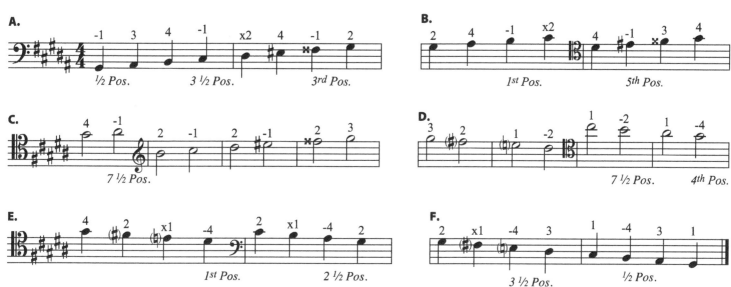

203 **G♯ MELODIC MINOR SCALE IN A TRADITIONAL PATTERN**—*Play the G♯ melodic minor scale in a traditional pattern at ♩ = 60. Add slurs as instructed by your teacher.*

204 **G♯ MINOR ARPEGGIO**—*Play the G♯ minor arpeggio at ♩ = 60.*

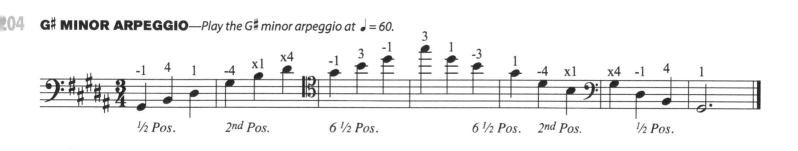

205 **G♯ MINOR ARPEGGIO IN A TRADITIONAL PATTERN**—*Play the G♯ minor arpeggio at ♩. = 60. Add slurs as instructed by your teacher.*

Level 4: Sound Scales and Arpeggios
A Major

(This is often required as an all-state audition scale.)

Check your fingering chart for finger placements. Mark in the half steps as directed by your teacher.

206   **A MAJOR SCALE**—*Learn the third octave of the A major scale.*

207   **A MAJOR SCALE SLURRED TWO PER BOW**—*Play the A major scale with two notes slurred per bow at ♩ = 60.*

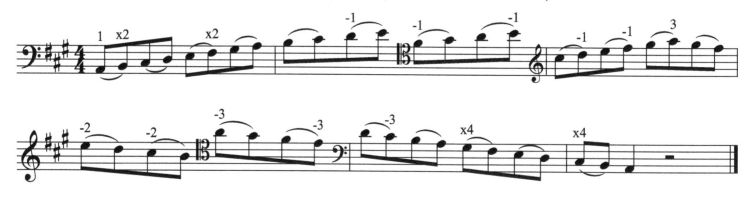

208   **A MAJOR SCALE SLURRED FOUR PER BOW**—*Play the A major scale in a traditional pattern with four notes slurred per bow at ♩ = 60.*

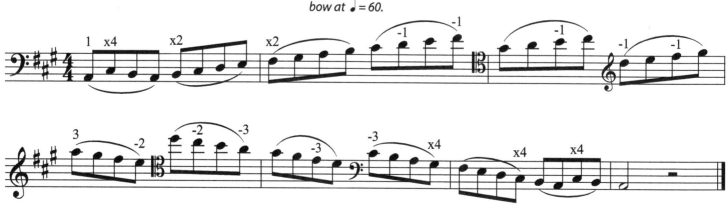

209 **A MAJOR ARPEGGIO**—*Learn the third octave of the A major arpeggio.*

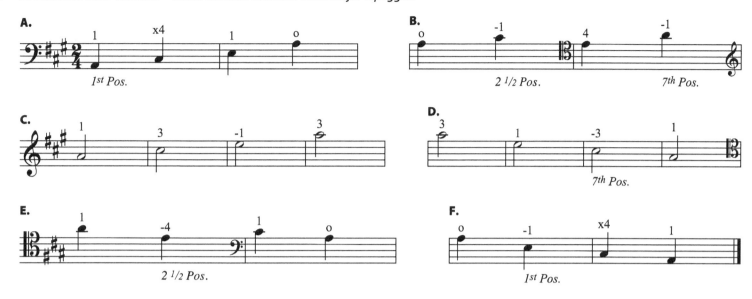

210 **A MAJOR ARPEGGIO IN QUARTER NOTES**—*Play the A major arpeggio at ♩ = 60.*

211 **A MAJOR ARPEGGIO SLURRED THREE PER BOW**—*Play the A major arpeggio with three notes slurred per bow at ♩. = 60.*

212 **A MAJOR SCALE ON ONE STRING**—*Play the A major scale on one string using one finger as indicated.*

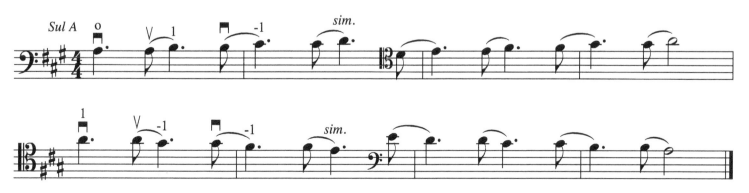

Level 4: Sound Scales and Arpeggios
A Melodic Minor

(This is often required as an all-state audition scale.)

Check your fingering chart for finger placements. Mark in the half steps as directed by your teacher.

213   **A MELODIC MINOR SCALE**—*Learn the third octave of the A melodic minor scale.*

214   **A MELODIC MINOR SCALE SLURRED TWO PER BOW**—*Play the A melodic minor scale with two notes slurred per bow at ♩ = 60.*

215   **A MELODIC MINOR SCALE SLURRED FOUR PER BOW**—*Play the A melodic minor scale in a traditional pattern with four notes slurred per bow at ♩ = 60.*

216 **A MINOR ARPEGGIO**—*Learn the third octave of the A minor arpeggio.*

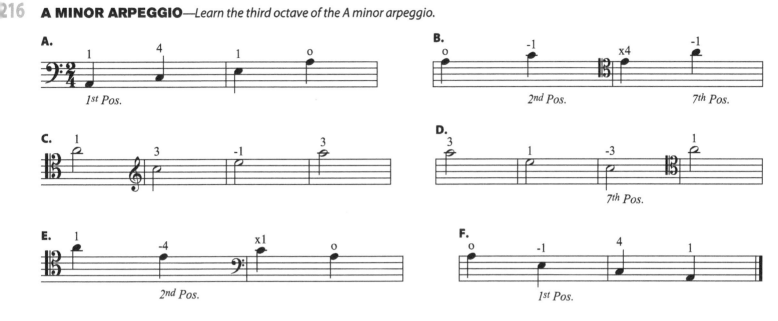

217 **A MINOR ARPEGGIO IN QUARTER NOTES**—*Play the A minor arpeggio at ♩ = 60.*

218 **A MINOR ARPEGGIO SLURRED THREE PER BOW**—*Play the A minor arpeggio with three notes slurred per bow at ♩. = 60.*

219 **A MELODIC MINOR SCALE ON ONE STRING**—*Play the A melodic minor scale on one string using one finger as indicated.*

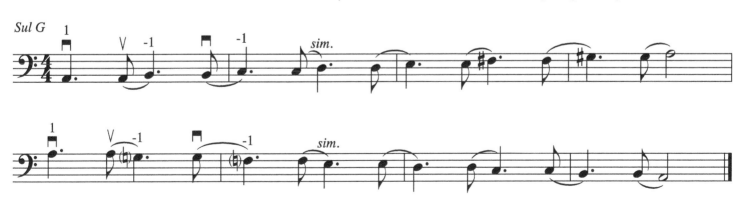

Level 4: Sound Scales and Arpeggios
B♭ Major

(This is often required as an all-state audition scale.)

Check your fingering chart for finger placements. Mark in the half steps as directed by your teacher.

220 B♭ **MAJOR SCALE**—*Learn the third octave of the B♭ major scale.*

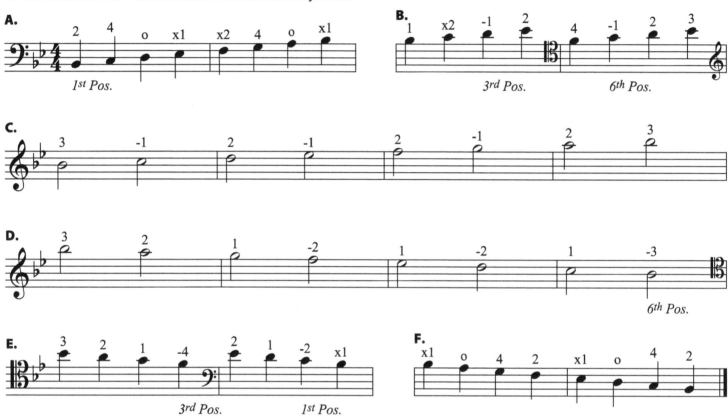

221 B♭ **MAJOR SCALE SLURRED TWO PER BOW**—*Play the B♭ major scale with two notes slurred per bow at ♩ = 60.*

222 B♭ **MAJOR SCALE SLURRED FOUR PER BOW**—*Play the B♭ major scale in a traditional pattern with four notes slurred per bow at ♩ = 60.*

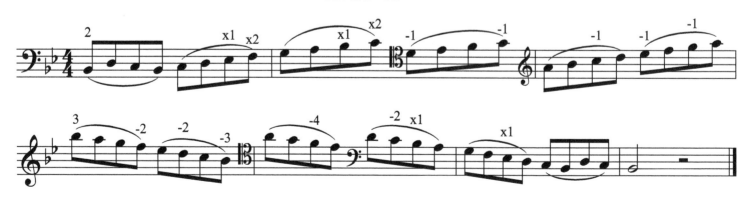

223 **B♭ MAJOR ARPEGGIO**—*Learn the third octave of the B♭ major arpeggio.*

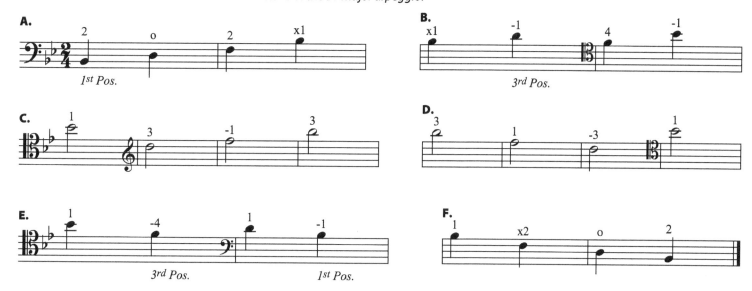

224 **B♭ MAJOR ARPEGGIO IN QUARTER NOTES**—*Play the B♭ major arpeggio at ♩ = 60.*

225 **B♭ MAJOR ARPEGGIO SLURRED THREE PER BOW**—*Play the B♭ major arpeggio with three notes slurred per bow at ♩. = 60.*

226 **B♭ MAJOR SCALE ON ONE STRING**—*Play the B♭ major scale on one string using one finger as indicated.*

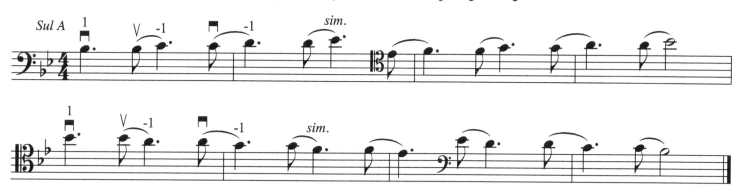

Level 4: Sound Scales and Arpeggios
B♭ Melodic Minor

Check your fingering chart for finger placements. Mark in the half steps as directed by your teacher.

227 B♭ **MELODIC MINOR SCALE**—*Learn the third octave of the B♭ melodic minor scale.*

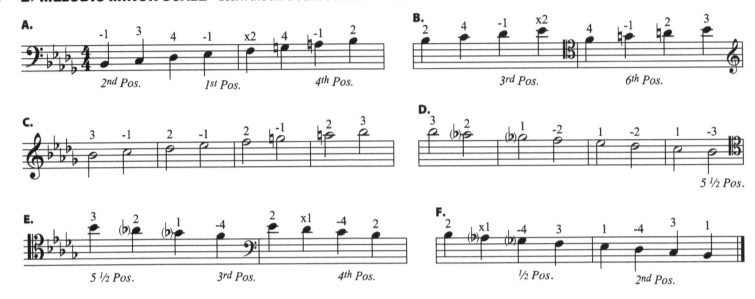

228 B♭ **MELODIC MINOR SCALE IN A TRADITIONAL PATTERN**—*Play the B♭ melodic minor scale in a traditional pattern at ♩ = 60. Add slurs as instructed by your teacher.*

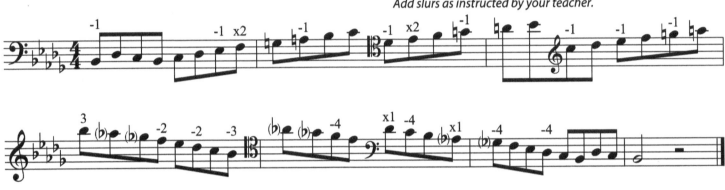

229 B♭ **MINOR ARPEGGIO**—*Play the B♭ minor arpeggio at ♩ = 60.*

230 B♭ **MINOR ARPEGGIO IN A TRADITIONAL PATTERN**—*Play the B♭ minor arpeggio at ♩. = 60. Add slurs as instructed by your teacher.*

Level 4: Sound Scales and Arpeggios
B Major

Check your fingering chart for finger placements. Mark in the half steps as directed by your teacher.

31 **B MAJOR SCALE**—*Learn the third octave of the B major scale.*

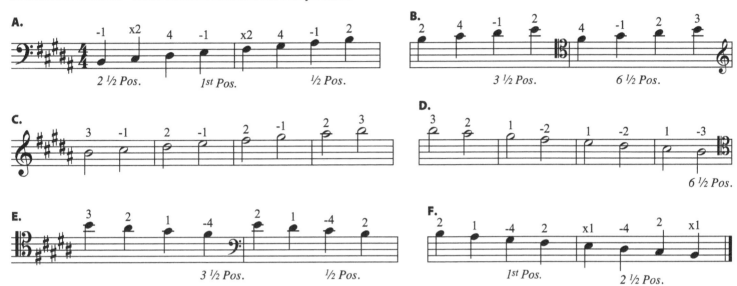

32 **B MAJOR SCALE IN A TRADITIONAL PATTERN**—*Play the B major scale in a traditional pattern at ♩ = 60. Add slurs as instructed by your teacher.*

33 **B MAJOR ARPEGGIO**—*Play the B major arpeggio at ♩ = 60.*

34 **B MAJOR ARPEGGIO IN A TRADITIONAL PATTERN**—*Play the B major arpeggio at ♩. = 60. Add slurs as instructed by your teacher.*

Level 4: Sound Scales and Arpeggios
B Melodic Minor

Check your fingering chart for finger placements. Mark in the half steps as directed by your teacher.

235 **B MELODIC MINOR SCALE**—*Learn the third octave of the B melodic minor scale.*

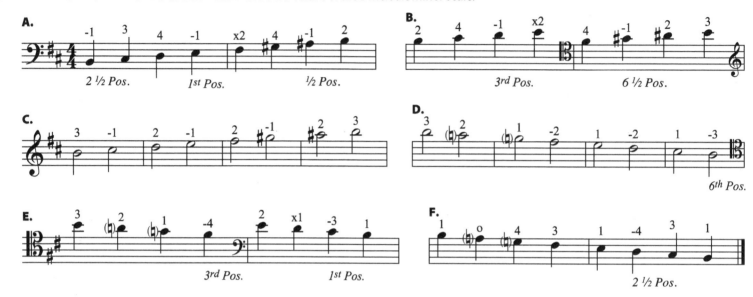

236 **B MELODIC MINOR SCALE IN A TRADITIONAL PATTERN**—*Play the B melodic minor scale in a traditional pattern at ♩ = 60.*
Add slurs as instructed by your teacher.

237 **B MINOR ARPEGGIO**—*Play the B minor arpeggio at ♩ = 60.*

238 **B MINOR ARPEGGIO IN A TRADITIONAL PATTERN**—*Play the B minor arpeggio at ♩. = 60. Add slurs as instructed by your teacher.*